D1568790

INVADERS FROM EARTH

INVASIVE MAMMAL SPECIES

Richard Spilsbury

PowerKiDS press™

New York

Published in 2015 by **The Rosen Publishing Group**
29 East 21st Street, New York, NY 10010

Library of Congress Cataloging-in-Publication Data

Spilsbury, Richard, 1963- author.
 Invasive mammal species / Richard Spilsbury.
      pages cm. – (Invaders from Earth)
 Includes bibliographical references and index.
 ISBN 978-1-4994-0060-1 (pbk.)
 ISBN 978-1-4994-0033-5 (6 pack)
 ISBN 978-1-4994-0058-8 (library binding)
 1. Introduced mammals–Juvenile literature. 2. Biological invasions–Juvenile literature.
 3. Environmental disasters–Juvenile literature. I. Title.
 QL606.S65 2015
 599.162–dc23

                            2014027647

Produced for Rosen by Calcium
Editors for Calcium: Sarah Eason and Robyn Hardyman
Designer: Paul Myerscough

Photo credits: Cover: Shutterstock: Eduard Kyslynskyy; Inside: Dreamstime: Annilein
24–25, Roberto Cerruti 25t, Isselee 13, Angelika Krikava 24, Dalia Kvedaraite 10–11,
Richie Lomba 15b, Filip Mráz 25b, Mario Radakovic 26–27, Bernhard Richter 20, Nancy
Riefenhauser 26t, Romantiche 17b, Christian Schmalhofer 12–13, Scottbeard 27b, Stephan
Morris 12t, Ivonne Wierink 27t; Shutterstock: Aerostato 17t, AFNR 4–5, Rebecca Anne 10,
Ryan M. Bolton 28–29, 29, Steve Bower 8, 9b, Linda Bucklin 5t, Neil Burton 21t, John
Carnemolla 5b, Cre8tive Images 19b, Terrance Emerson 4t, Erni 7t, Bonnie Fink 8–9,
Matt Gibson 2–3, 22, 22–23, 30–31, 32, Gopause 19t, Arto Hakola 9t, Mark Higgins 11tr,
Budimir Jevtic 20–21, Kajornyot 18, Kavram 16–17, Heiko Kiera 6–7, 6b, Alis Leonte 7b,
Paul Maguire 11tl, Stephen Meese 28b, Patrik Mezirka 14, Milosz M 28t, Nelik 14–15,
Eduardo Rivero 23t, Seawhisper 15t, Eugene Sim 18–19, Taviphoto 23b, UbjsP 1, 16, Andrius
Vaicikonis 12b, Zorandim 21b.

Manufactured in the United States of America

CPSIA Compliance Information: Batch CW15PK: For Further Information contact
Rosen Publishing, New York, New York at 1-800-237-9932

CONTENTS

WHAT ARE MAMMAL INVADERS?

COWS

Mammal **invaders** are **mammals** that arrive in a new place and start to live and **reproduce** there. Some invaders are useful, but others harm wildlife, people, and even the new places where they live.

Traveling Mammals

Most mammal invaders were moved to new places by people. For example, people introduced animals like cows and rabbits to eat them. They introduced cats to kill rats and other pests. Other mammals arrived by accident. For example, rats that climbed onto ships to find food were carried to new places.

Unwelcome Visitors

The dodo was a bird that became **extinct** in the 1600s. It died out partly because it was eaten by dogs and cats that were introduced to its **habitat**. **Invasive species** often cause harm in other ways, too. They take food and space that **native** animals need, or they spread diseases.

DODO

The dingo was an Asian wild dog that was introduced to Australia by people a long time ago.

EARTH UNDER ATTACK

Some species we think are native were actually invaders in the past. For example, today dingoes are found in Australia, but they are **descendants** of wild dogs that were introduced to Australia by Asian sailors 4,000 years ago!

5

RAT

There are rats almost everywhere in the world. Rats succeed because they are tough, reproduce quickly, and eat a wide variety of foods.

Passage from Asia

Rats are native to Asia. They spread throughout the world mostly as unwanted passengers on ships. Rats also traveled short distances by swimming. Rats mostly live underground in burrows, tunnels, and sewers. They usually live near people, because we supply them with food.

Rats have long, tough teeth that can bite through metal. Their teeth grow constantly.

RAT EATING
GRAIN

Ominous Omnivores

Rats are pests. They eat stored foods such as wheat or rice. They also spread diseases by carrying the germs they pick up in sewers or from waste food. Rats are bad news for wild animals, too. They kill and eat anything from insects and **reptiles** to birds. They especially like to eat birds' eggs.

INVADER ANALYSIS

One-third of all seabird species that nest on islands are under threat from rat invaders. Those at most risk, such as storm petrels and shearwaters, nest underground in burrows, just like rats.

RAT PUPS IN A NEST

NINE-BANDED ARMADILLO

The body of the nine-banded armadillo is covered in bony, armorlike plates. This tough cookie can march for miles. It can also hold its breath underwater for up to 6 minutes, while it swims or walks along the bottom of a river.

Spreading North

Armadillos are native to South America, but they have slowly moved into southern parts of the United States. People made it easier for the armadillos to spread by hunting the **predators** that killed them, such as black bears and coyotes. When people took water from rivers for their crops, the rivers became shallower and much easier for armadillos to cross.

NINE-BANDED ARMADILLO

EARTH UNDER ATTACK

Nine-banded armadillos are active at night, when they burrow and feed. They use their sense of smell to find food in the ground. They eat mainly insects and **invertebrates**, which they dig up with their sharp claws.

SHARP CLAWS

The nine-banded armadillo's tough body armor helps protect it from hungry predators.

Armadillo Attack

Armadillos are a problem because the burrows that they dig cause soil **erosion**. They can even damage buildings. Armadillos also feed on eggs from the nests of **endangered** turtles, such as loggerheads. They dig and damage backyards, sports fields, and other properties, and they also spread disease.

WILD RABBIT

Rabbits are one of the world's worst mammal invaders. In many countries, their **overgrazing** is making some plants rare, which means there is less food for wild animals and farm animals to eat.

Population Explosion

In 1859, a visiting Englishman released 24 wild rabbits in Australia, so he and his friends could hunt them. A century later, there were more than 600 million rabbits in Australia. That is because they can reproduce from the age of 8 months and can have 30 babies each year.

Rabbits have long ears and eyes on the side of their heads, to help them hear and see danger.

RABBIT

RABBIT-PROOF FENCE

Battling the Bunnies

People try to stop the spread of rabbits but without success. They build fences to keep them off their land, but the rabbits just burrow under them. They introduce cats and foxes to catch the rabbits, but these also kill rare native animals.

EARTH UNDER ATTACK

Rabbits are native to southern Europe and northwest Africa. They spread because people kept them for food. They kept rabbits in large outside burrows or in cages, and some escaped into the wild. Rabbits were also released into the wild on deserted islands, so that any shipwrecked sailors would find food and stay alive!

STOAT

Stoats look furry and friendly, but these short-tailed animals will attack creatures much bigger than themselves. They also kill many birds and small mammals.

The Story of Stoats

Stoats are native to Europe, parts of Asia, and North America. They were introduced to countries such as New Zealand to kill smaller invasive animals, like rabbits. Instead, they became a major predator of native animals. They caused several bird species to become extinct.

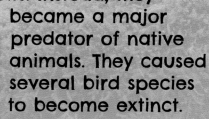

STOAT IN WINTER

Kiwi Killers

Stoats can reach nests in small holes and high up in trees to eat the eggs and chicks inside them. The national bird of New Zealand, the kiwi, is in great danger from predators because it cannot fly. Stoats eat up to 4,000 kiwi chicks each year. To stop this, people have set up kiwi nurseries to protect kiwi chicks.

Stoats are difficult to see in the wild because they are small, secretive, and move fast.

KIWI

INVADER ANALYSIS

Stoats can swim up to 1 mile (1.6 km) in water, and can travel 40 miles (64.3 km) across land in one trip. They kill as much prey as they can and store any food that they cannot immediately eat.

GRAY SQUIRREL

Gray squirrels look fluffy and cute, but in the United Kingdom, these bushy-tailed creatures are deadly villains because they have helped kill off the native red squirrels.

Death by Disease

In the late 1800s, a few people released pairs of American gray squirrels in the United Kingdom, because they thought they looked cute. However, gray squirrels carry a disease called squirrel pox, which kills red squirrels but does not harm grays. When red squirrels die, gray squirrels take over the woodlands where the reds lived.

Scientists are currently developing a medicine to stop the squirrel disease from killing red squirrels in the United Kingdom.

RED SQUIRREL

At one time, red squirrels were the only squirrel in the United Kingdom. Now there are about 3 million gray squirrels there and only about 120,000 red squirrels.

Taking Over

Gray squirrels are twice the weight of red squirrels. They eat seven times more food per acre (ha), so they outcompete the reds for food. Fewer red squirrels are born, and young reds struggle to survive, so their numbers decline. Gray squirrels can also cause damage to woodlands, crops, and backyards.

GRAY SQUIRREL

WILD GOAT

Goats are shaggy eating machines! They can easily strip all the leaves from trees and bushes in one place before moving on to another.

Going Wild

Wild goats from Asia were first kept by people for their meat, milk, and skins around 10,000 years ago. These products have become so popular that goats are now kept worldwide. However, in many places, domestic goats have escaped, reproduced, and become wild once more.

PLANT EATER

Goats can even climb up trees to reach leaves!

The Goat Threat

Goats will eat any plant, from grasses and tree twigs to seaweed and ferns. A large herd can easily overgraze land. This has a bigger impact when the land has few plants or crops, or when the area is small, such as on islands. Overgrazing has threatened wild plants and the animals that rely on them all over the world.

WILD GOAT

INVADER ANALYSIS

Goats **have** sharp, cutting tee**th** in **their** lower jaws **that bite** against a bony **pad** in **their** upper jaws. **They have** large stomachs that can **hold** a lot of food. **Their** stomach contains bacteria **that help** break down tough plant food.

LONG-TAILED MACAQUE

Long-tailed macaques are native to Southeast Asia, but they have been introduced into Mauritius, Palau, Hong Kong, and parts of Indonesia. In these places they are causing the decline of many bird species, because they compete with them for food.

Leaping for Lunch

Long-tailed macaques can leap up to 16 feet (5 m) between trees, using their long tails for balance, as they search for fruit and leaves. This robs local birds of food.

LONG-TAILED MACAQUE AND BABY

Long-tailed macaques were introduced to Mauritius by Portuguese explorers in the Indian Ocean in the early 1600s. Because they have no natural predators on the island, their numbers have grown. Today, about 35,000 live there!

The long-tailed macaque's tail is often longer than its whole body and head combined.

GREEN PARROT

Bird Losses

On Mauritius, long-tailed macaques have caused the near extinction of several bird species, including the beautiful green parrot. They destroy birds' nests as they move through the treetops, and sometimes they also eat the eggs of endangered bird species.

WILD HOG

Spanish explorers brought hogs, or pigs, to the United States for food. Over time, some escaped and formed wild populations. Today, they cause severe damage to wildlife and habitats.

Hungry Hogs

Wild hogs use their extra-long snouts to root as deep as 3 feet (1 m) into the ground to search for plants, worms, and insects. They eat large amounts of food, which makes it tough for other wildlife to survive. Their digging also erodes the soil, which stops new plants from growing and disturbs birds that make their nests on the ground.

Wild hogs wallow in mud to cool down. This makes the water in ponds and **wetlands** too muddy for fish, and it destroys plants.

Farmers' Foe

Wild hogs eat fields of crops such as wheat, potatoes, melons, and grass. They move up and down the rows of crops, until every plant is eaten or damaged. The hogs eat foods put out for farm animals and sometimes even eat baby animals such as lambs and calves. They also spread diseases to farm animals. These diseases may be passed on to humans in undercooked meat.

LONG SNOUT

WILD HOG AND PIGLETS

INVADER ANALYSIS

One reason **wild hogs spread so easily is that they reproduce fast.** Young hogs can **begin to have** young from 6 months old. Females can **give birth to up to eight piglets, twice a year.**

21

RED DEER

Red deer are native to Europe and Asia, but they have caused problems for other wildlife since being introduced to North and South America, New Zealand, and Australia.

Grass Grazers

Red deer were introduced to new places as food or to be hunted for sport. However, they soon spread. They eat grass, and a lot of it. In some places red deer are outcompeting native species. In northern Chile and Argentina, they outcompete an endangered deer and the guanaco, a South American llama.

Red deer eat all kinds of plants including grasses, berries, and mosses.

Adaptable Deer

Red deer are **adaptable** so they can live in a variety of habitats, including grasslands and mountains. Large populations of grazing deer can cause soil erosion. This stops some native plants from growing and changes the habitat. People try to control the red deer by hunting it.

GUANACO

TREE BARK

INVADER ANALYSIS

In **Australia's Royal National Park,** parts of the forest where many red deer live have up to 70 percent fewer plant species than nearby areas with fewer deer. The deer even strip the bark from trees.

COYPU

Coypus are sometimes called river rats, because their long tails make them look like giant rats. These rodents are a pest, just like their smaller cousin, the rat.

Rat Ranches

Coypus are native to South America, but were introduced to Europe, North America, and Asia by ranchers who raised them for their fur. Coypus that escaped from the fur farms reproduced in the wild and spread widely. They live near rivers and marshes. They are destroying these and other wetlands because of their feeding habits, nests, and burrows.

An adult coypu's big front teeth are orange because they contain iron. The iron makes the teeth tough and hard.

EARTH UNDER ATTACK

In Japan, coypus threaten an endangered dragonfly and the deep-bodied bitterling fish. In Italy, coypus have destroyed the water lilies that grew on wetlands and provided shelter in which birds called whiskered terns can reproduce.

COYPU

COYPU FAMILY

Wetland Destroyers

Coypus dig long tunnels through wetlands, eroding river banks and damaging the marshes. Their large, gnawing teeth help them eat many plants, turning marshlands full of plants into areas of empty, open water. This is a great loss because wetlands are important habitats for many species of plants and animals that cannot live anywhere else.

CAT

Cats are one of our best-loved pets but, make no mistake, they are also killers.

CAT HUNTING

Catastrophic Cats

Cats were first kept by people to kill troublesome rats and mice. Today, cats are having a huge impact on many rarer wild animals, especially birds. For example, the 60 million wild cats in the United States are thought to kill around 480 million birds each year.

EARTH UNDER ATTACK

Small wild cats were first kept as pets around 2000 BC, in ancient Egypt. They were carried through Europe by the Romans. In later centuries, they spread to the rest of the world on ships during voyages of discovery and trade. In many places there are bands of wild and stray cats that are the descendants of ancient pet cats.

Assassin's Weapons

The cat is made for hunting. It has large forward-facing eyes that can see well in the day and at night. Its ears can turn 180 degrees to track sounds. It has large, pointed teeth and needle-sharp claws to help it catch prey. Cats can leap five times their own height to make a kill, too.

BIRD THREAT

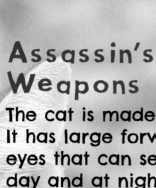

Cats hunt their prey by moving slowly and quietly until they are close to their victim. Then they pounce!

STOPPING INVASIONS

Invasive species are a huge problem. People can help habitats and native species by removing existing animal invaders and by preventing new ones from arriving.

Targeting the Invaders

People get rid of invaders by killing them or moving them elsewhere. For example, in Australia brush-tailed rock wallabies are rare because foxes kill their young. People help the wallabies survive by poisoning the foxes. However, using poison is dangerous because it can affect pet animals, too.

Fox poison in Australia contains chemicals similar to those found in native plants, which do not harm the animals that eat them.

WALLABY

28

No New Arrivals

Another way to stop invaders is to check places where they usually arrive. For example, Anchorage, Alaska, is the only rat-free port in the world, because all arriving ships are carefully checked for rats. Governments can also tell people not to release their pets into the wild, or fine the owners if they do.

EARTH UNDER ATTACK

When native giant tortoises on the famous Galapagos Islands began to die because invasive goats were eating too many plants, people hunted the goats. However, some remained hidden, so people released some goats wearing radio collars and they joined the hiding goats. Scientists tracked the signals from the collars to find and destroy the goats.

GIANT TORTOISE

GLOSSARY

adaptable Adjusts to new situations.

bacteria Tiny things that can cause disease.

descendants Plants or animals directly related to plants or animals that lived in the past.

endangered In danger of dying out completely.

erosion The wearing away of soil.

extinct Died out completely.

habitat A place where an animal or plant lives.

invaders Things that spread quickly and cause harm.

invasive species A living thing that does not belong to an area and can harm it.

invertebrates Animals without backbones.

mammals Animals that have some hair on their bodies and give birth to live young.

native Born in or belonging to a place.

overgrazing Eating too many plants in an area.

predators Animals that hunt and eat other animals.

prey An animal that is hunted and eaten by other animals.

reproduce To produce babies.

reptiles Animals that lay eggs, have scaly or hard skin, and are cold-blooded.

wetlands Lands that are always wet.